MW00354547

The BAD DAY BOOK

The BAD DAY BOOK

Robyn Freedman Spizman and Tracy Green

Illustrations by John Knorr

LONGSTREET PRESS
Atlanta, Georgia

Published by
LONGSTREET PRESS, INC.
A subsidiary of Cox Newspapers,
A division of Cox Enterprises, Inc.
2140 Newmarket Parkway
Suite 118
Marietta, GA 30067

Text copyright © 1994 by Robyn Freedman Spizman and Tracy Green
Illustrations copyright © 1994 by John Knorr

All rights reserved. No part of this book may be reproduced in any form or by any means without the prior written permission of the Publisher, excepting brief quotations used in connection with reviews, written specifically for inclusion in a magazine or newspaper.

Printed in the United States of America

1st printing 1994

Library of Congress Catalog Card Number: 93-81149
ISBN 1-56352-140-7

This book was printed by Data Reproductions Corporation, Rochester Hills, Michigan.

Cover illustration by John Knorr
Cover design by Jill Dible
Book design by Laura McDonald

This book is dedicated to anyone who has ever had a

bad day . . . and gotten over it.

Good-Day People We Want to Thank

Maegan Ahern, Lois Blonder, Cindy Bosilkov, Bettye Storne,

Ryan Cameron, Chad Foster, Jack Freedman, Phyllis Freedman,

Karin Green, Richard Green, Gail Heyman, Rusty Johnson,

Bert Paisley, Mark Shavin, Marla Shavin, Willy Spizman,

Suzanne Comer Bell, and Chuck Perry

BAD DAY \bad dāy\ *adj., noun.* **1:** A day you would like to forget. A day or moment in that day which causes the entire day to be a disaster. Almost always a day you had expected to go very well or at least okay. **2:** A psychologically profound day that temporarily changes the way you look at things, or yourself. **3:** Generally referred to as stinking, rotten, or a bummer. Frequently followed by a speedy return to bed with the covers pulled over the head. (Note: Common to all Homo sapiens.)

"You won't believe what a BAD DAY I've had!"

How many times in your life have you said that? We've all said it. Well, the idea of this book is to celebrate the inevitability of the bad day, and the beautiful, ironic notion that no matter what a bad day may bring, life always surprises us down the road with a good one. We hope that as we all make our way through life's fragile, patience-testing moments, a little humor will help us along in the journey.

So, here's to your very best bad days! May the craziest of them become the ones you look back on and laugh.

Bad-Day Warning Signs

Check this list. If two or more of these things happen to you before 10:00 a.m., look out—you're on your way to the cover of *Bad-Day Magazine*!

You wake up late.

You swear at the alarm clock because you woke up late.

You swear at your spouse because you woke up late.

Your spouse swears back at you because it was your own fault to begin with.

Your shower water is ice cold.

You spill your coffee.

You run your pantyhose.

You've lost your wallet.

You've lost your keys.

You're worried that you've lost your mind.

Your child announces he needs two dozen cupcakes
for school today.

You step in gum.

You step in something worse than gum.

A stranger says, "Wow . . . are you having a bad hair
day, or what?"

You can't button the top button on your pants.

You discover a new face wrinkle.

Your friend points out the wrinkle (just in case you missed it!).

Your boss introduces you to a new co-worker who appears to be younger, better-looking and more energetic than you are.

The new co-worker says, "It's so funny, the boss and I are pals from way back. By the way, what's with your hair?"

True-Life Bad Days

So you think you've had a bad day? Here's a sampling of bad days as told to us by the folks who survived them! Some are funny, some are ironic, some are just plain classic bad days! Ages, by the way, refer to when they had the bad day (most are now older and wiser). See if any of your bad days stack up to these:

My husband called me Linda during our wedding vows. My name is Liz. He said he was nervous. — **age 28**

A neighbor's child I was baby-sitting for got his head stuck between the rungs on our stair railing. — **age 16**

I threw up on the first day of kindergarten in front of the other kids. — **age 5**

I rode my bike 110 miles to my old girlfriend's house to show her I loved her enough to win her back. When I got there, her Mom said she was out of town with her new boyfriend. Her Dad drove me (and my bike) home in his van.

— **age 17**

I fainted during my own Bar Mitzvah. — **age 13**

I was fired from my job on my birthday. — **age 49**

AND LAYING HIS FINGER ASIDE OF HIS NOSE...

I was playing Santa at a small store for the holidays. I got in a fistfight with the manager, and he threw me out of the store in front of the kids, without paying me. I had to walk home, in the rain, in the red suit. — **age 21**

My capped front tooth flew out of my mouth while
I was giving a speech. It actually deflected right off the
notebook of a woman in the front row. — **age 27**

I was invited to sing at a big amateur
contest in New York City. All my friends drove
up with me. I was booed off the stage after
90 seconds. — **age 22**

I got an obscene phone call and the caller
knew my name. — **age 41**

I took cupcakes out of my freezer and frosted
them with chocolate frosting for my daughter's
birthday party. When the kids bit into them, we
realized they were corn muffins. — **age 31**

BE SYMPATHETIC.
IT'S PROBABLY THE FATHER OF THE BRIDE.

Ten guests were mugged outside my wedding party.
All of their jewelry, including wedding rings,
was stolen. — **age 22**

We took the whole family, including my grandmother, to visit the Statue of Liberty and accidentally left her there. I thought she was with my sister, and vice versa. We had to catch the ferry back to get her. — **age 31**

I was the one-in-a-million person who had to attempt to parallel park during my driver's exam. — **age 16**

I exposed my entire birthday party to chicken pox. — **age 6**

I locked my keys in the car, with the car running, at 10:00 p.m. on Christmas night. You don't even want to know how much I had to pay a locksmith to come help me. — **age 32**

We took our five-year-old on his first boat trip.
He threw the keys to our car overboard into
Lake Superior. — **age 30**

HOLD ON. YOU CAN TAKE A TWO-CLUB-LENGTH DROP.

I had a garden wedding at a golf and tennis country club. During the vows, my wife-to-be was knocked almost unconscious by a golf ball. We eventually continued with the wedding, but looking back, I wonder if it was a sign since we were divorced thirteen months later. — **age 42**

I stepped in a fire-ant hill, barefoot. — **age 9**

On my wedding day, we put my dress in the car and drove to the church. When we got to the church, we realized the skirt of the gown was shut into the greasy hinge of the door. I walked down the aisle with a big crease of grease right down the side of the gown. — **age 22**

I momentarily forgot my boss's name when introducing him. —**age 20**

I was driving carpool and a very carsick
child started a chain reaction with the other
kids, if you get my drift. — **age 31**

I went to the airport to pick up my parents
and noticed a man kissing and hugging a woman
on the moving sidewalk. When they got closer
I realized it was the man I had been dating.
Dating up until that moment, I guess I
should say. —**age 27**

MADAM, I'M USUALLY TIPPED HANDSOMELY FOR ACHIEVING THAT LOOK.

My hairdresser gave me a "perm" that fried my hair so bad,

he didn't even make me pay for it. — **age 26**

Our two-year-old flushed his Ninja Turtle down the toilet to "return it to the sewer." The toilet had to be replaced. — **age 31**

My boyfriend proposed on top of Stone Mountain, Georgia. I threw my arms around him as I said yes and knocked an antique diamond ring out of his hand, over the edge. We never found it. —**age 24**

We drove six hours in the wrong direction on vacation. — **age 52**

I tripped coming down the stairs at high school graduation. —age 18

This obnoxious young woman at work said to me,
"You're lucky. You have such a nice face, you can get away
with not watching your weight." — **age 42**

My mom made me get a "pixie" haircut and when I got to
school all the kids said I looked like a boy. — **age 6**

I went on a blind date and when I picked
her up, I recognized her as a receptionist I had
recently fired. — **age 32**

In the middle of our thirtieth-anniversary
dinner party, two police cars and an ambulance
arrived in our driveway. Our young grandson
had dialed 911. — **age 51**

The first time I visited a psychiatrist, he fell
asleep during our session. — **age 24**

AN' WOULD YOU LIKE TO HEAR THE GREETING DAD USES WHEN HE WAVES?

My son's teacher called me at work because my son was spending the day in "time out" for "flipping the bird" to her. He told the teacher it was "a wave my Dad does when he drives." — **age 44**

I sat on a big plate of food at the company

cookout. — **age 53**

I got on a plane for New York for the most
important two-day business trip of my career.
I realized somewhere over Pennsylvania that I'd
left my bag and briefcase in the gate area
back at the airport. — **age 26**

In art class, we all put our final pottery
projects in the kiln together. Apparently mine
had an airhole because it exploded in the
kiln and burst everybody else's
final projects. — **age 15**

MY CHRISTMAS. WE WENT SHOPPING.
MOMMY SAID: "✳✳▱✦☆△◎✳"
DADDY SAID: "☆✳✳✪⬠◎✳!"
MOMMY SAID: "OK, YOU'RE NOT GETTIN' ANY"
DADDY SAID: "SO WHAT ELSE IS NEW?"
BUT MOMMY DIDN'T MEAN IT 'CAUSE
THERE WERE PRESENTS FOR
DADDY UNDER THE TREE ANYWAY.

Our seven-year-old read a Christmas story to her
class detailing the argument her mother and I had while
Christmas shopping at the mall. — **age 34**

I was on a sight-seeing helicopter flight in Hawaii and we had to make a frightening emergency landing. — **age 62**

My car broke down
on a deserted stretch
of asphalt highway, in
Georgia, in July.
— age 25

I gave a speech to my French class without knowing the tail of my shirt was sticking out the front of my fly. — **age 16**

My sister told my prom date, "Guess what? He has a big box of *Playboys* under his bed." — **age 17**

On my wedding day, my groomsmen wrote "Just Married" all over my GTO in shaving cream. The next day, the paint on the car came off with it. — **age 21**

I went for a beauty makeover at the mall.
When I came home and walked in to my
four-year-old son's room he said, "Oooh, Mom,
I think your face is gonna scare my fish."

— age 40

On my thirtieth birthday, I was giggling
all day because I was absolutely sure my wife
had organized a huge surprise party for me.
She hadn't. She ordered Chinese food and
gave me one of those Wet Vac machines
as a gift. **— age 30**

My husband took me to the dog track and went bananas
when he won! But it was my first time to the track and I had
inadvertently thrown out the winning ticket. — **age 43**

Our wedding photographer's car was
stolen with all of our wedding pictures and
negatives in the trunk. — **age 24**

I started dating a great guy named Mick, but
didn't tell him I also had a romantic relationship
back home. I decided it was time to send a
"Dear John" letter to my home-town guy.
I guess my mind was on Mick — he called
when he received the letter. I had accidentally
mailed it to *him*! But he forgave me and
married me. — **age 23**

SO YOU'RE THE BOSS...
WELL, I'M SUPPOSED TO
POLISH THE
OL' APPLE.

I took a blind date to my company holiday party. She drank too much wine and made jokes to my (balding) boss about the Hair Club for Men.

— **age 29**

After my high school reunion, a gorgeous single guy from our class called me for lunch. Of course I was thrilled. But at the lunch he tried to sell me insurance. — **age 28**

A clothing boutique saleswoman talked me into trying on a miniskirt. The zipper got stuck and they had to call a seamstress to come and help get me out of it. — **age 40**

I THINK
IT'S AN OMEN.

We cut the cake at our wedding
and the whole thing
split in half! — **age 28**

I was pushing my cart at the grocery store and crashed into a big red-wine display. — **age 45**

My wife and I saw Tommy Lasorda in the L.A. airport and she said, "My husband always says you're a loud-mouth but I always tell him it takes one to know one!" — **age 56**

My son tried to cook popcorn in the pressure cooker. — **age 34**

I had a dinner party and unknowingly invited a dinner guest's ex-wife and her new husband to the same dinner. — **age 49**

My shoelace got caught in the mall escalator. — **age 11**

A guest had a panic attack at our wedding reception. The paramedics took him out on a stretcher. — **age 24**

Our daughter lost her first tooth, put it under her pillow, and we completely forgot to replace it with magical money. We told her the tooth fairy was on vacation. — **age 28**

Our son's camp counselor called us from
summer sleep-away camp. He said our boy was
the only child left at camp—we thought camp
lasted one more day! Our son seemed to think
it was sort of funny but the counselor
did not. — **age 39**

My husband and I were walking into a party
hosted by his old girlfriend. I was nervous, and
he was trying to be sweet. As he helped me with
my coat he said, "Honey, in that outfit you really
remind me of my mom." — **age 27**

I heard my three-year-old daughter tell my wife, "It's funny having a fat Dad! — **age 35**

I popped two steaks into the oven broiler and asked my
girlfriend to take them out when they were ready, while I ran back
to the store. I came home to find a firetruck at my house. She said,
"I smelled them burning but every time I opened the oven door,
there was nothing in there! — **age 22**

A guy whom I'd been dating invited
me to spend a cozy night at a mountain cabin. I
told him I would go if I could have my own
room (just to test his intentions). He said that
would be fine. After a warm and romantic
dinner by firelight, he made me stick
to the deal! — **age 30**

I planned a huge surprise party for a friend
and he showed up wearing a T-shirt that said,
"Welcome to My Surprise Party: The Worst
Kept Secret in Town" — **age 34**

We thought we heard squirrels in our attic. I woke up to
find one sitting on my headboard. — **age 61**

I had two parking lot fender-benders in
one afternoon. — **age 17**

Boiling pasta for company, I spotted lots of tiny
bugs floating on top. — **age 31**

In college, I was incredibly nervous while I
gave a speech. I looked down most of the time,
and talked very fast. But I got through it! When
I got back to my seat, the girl next to me said,
"Congratulations. You made a complete ass
out of yourself." — **age 20**

When I left the house on a freezing day, my car hit a patch of ice and slid into my living room window. — **age 33**

I went fly fishing with a great guy, so I was trying to show him what a cool outdoors-woman I could be. First I fell in the river up to my armpits, then I screamed upstream, "Come help me land this fish!" when it turned out to be a record-setting weed. —**age 31**

I was boiling eggs and forgot about them until they blew up! —age 20

The worst surprise spring snowstorm in Georgia history ruined my March wedding. — **age 24**

Sixteen years old, and my parents gave me a plane ticket to go visit a girl I'd struck up a long-distance "puppy love" romance with. But when I got there, she made it clear she was dating another big, handsome guy. I said, "So, where do I fit in?" and she said, "You don't." It's twenty years later and I hate to admit it, but I don't think you ever get over a moment like that. — **age 16**

The day of an important job interview, I
woke up with a gigantic blemish right under my
eye. I mean huge. It was all I could think about
during the interview, and I could tell the
interviewer was looking at the top of my head
rather than looking me in the eye, so it wouldn't
look like he was staring at it. Big surprise . . .
I didn't get the job. — **age 22**

Lying on the beach in Jamaica with my
husband, he says, "Honey, I love you but you're
too old for that bikini." — **age 38**

I dropped the Thanksgiving turkey off the platter as I was parading into the dining room with it. — **age 40**

I went to a plastic surgeon to ask him
about getting a nose job. He recommended
not only a nose job but my eyes, chin,
and neck. — **age 43**

I took my girlfriend out for New Year's Eve,
an expensive dinner, and dancing to a big band
at a fancy hotel. On the way home in the cab,
she broke up with me. I said, "Thanks for
letting me go broke before you broke that
news to me." — **age 25**

IF IT BOUNCES IT MEANS IT'S DONE.

I dropped the Thanksgiving turkey off the platter as I was
parading into the dining room with it. — **age 40**

I went to a plastic surgeon to ask him
about getting a nose job. He recommended
not only a nose job but my eyes, chin,
and neck. — **age 43**

I took my girlfriend out for New Year's Eve,
an expensive dinner, and dancing to a big band
at a fancy hotel. On the way home in the cab,
she broke up with me. I said, "Thanks for
letting me go broke before you broke that
news to me." — **age 25**

I lost my engagement ring on a three-mile beach walk.

— age 63

The police returned our stolen car . . . with bullet holes
in it. — **age 48**

I was saying goodnight to this woman at the end of our first date. I said, "I need to get your number again, I misplaced it." She said, "You won't be needing my number. Good night."

— **age 26**

I got my big break by being interviewed on the local TV sports news. However, they not only misspelled my first name but used someone else's last name. — **age 46**

I got up my nerve to say "I love you" to a new
boyfriend. He said, "Thanks." — **age 29**

My car was broken into on Christmas Eve,
and they stole my winter coat and the presents I
was bringing to my family. — **age 28**

Running up a flight of stairs to give my first
big presentation at work, I tripped and tore out
the shoulder seam in my suit coat. I had to give
that presentation looking more like a bum
than a future executive. — **age 23**

In sixth grade, my twin brother told all his friends that
I had my first period. — **age 11**

I went to the college health center with bad abdominal pain. They mistakenly diagnosed me as pregnant, and called my parents with the diagnosis. — **age 18**

I worked for one year writing a book and saved it on the computer. A virus infected all the files and I had to salvage the book by piecing together all the chapters from the copies I had saved. — **age 40**

I lost my wedding band in the ocean on the second day of our honeymoon. — **age 25**

My wife and I both got fed up and quit our jobs on the same afternoon without consulting each other first! Dinner that night was pretty interesting. — **age 37**

My wife says, "Don't wear your tuxedo to this party. Nobody else will be wearing one, you'd feel funny in a tuxedo." So, of course, I wore a light-colored suit and was the only man in the room not wearing a tux. — **age 34**

I wrote a nasty letter to my teacher, but didn't plan on sending it. My father mailed it accidentally. — **age 14**

The Ultimate Recurring Bad Day: Our family was in Olympia, Washington, when Mount St. Helen's erupted, Fresno for the Coalinga earthquake, South Florida for Hurricane Floyd, San Francisco for the 1989 earthquake, and Oakland, California, for the big fires. Do not accept an invitation to vacation with us.

Bad Day Note

That last bad-day story comes from the collection of Ed Mauss and his "Hard Luck Gazette." He considers himself a "magnet for misfortune," so he puts out a monthly newsletter about hard luck and bad days. A subscription to the newsletter is $30 a year. You can get a free introductory copy by calling 714-831-7419, or write to Ed at:

"Hard Luck Gazette"
123 Briarwood Lane
Aliso Viejo, CA 92656

If you've had a bad day you'd like
to share with us, send it to:

"The Bad Day Book"
LONGSTREET PRESS
2140 Newmarket Parkway, Suite 118
Marietta, GA 30067

Twenty Books to Help You Through a Bad Day

Feeling Good: The New Mood Therapy, by Dr. David Burns (Avon).
Learn to take charge of the mood swings a bad day can bring.

7 Habits of Highly Effective People, by Stephen Covey (Simon &
Schuster). Bad-day problem-solving help.

The Book of Questions, by Gregory Stock (Workman). Clear out
your bad-day brain with fresh questions, from the curious to the
crazy to the serious.

A Light in the Attic, by Shel Silverstein (HarperCollins). A whimsi-
cal detour for a bad day.

Meditations from the Road, by M. Scott Peck (Simon & Schuster).
Daily wisdom for a bad day from the "Road Less Travelled."

Live and Learn and Pass It On, by H. Jackson Brown, Jr. (Rutledge-Hill). A collection of delightful lessons learned, filled with wisdom sure to prevent bad days from happening!

The Battery Book, by Joey Reiman (Longstreet). An instant charge-up when a bad day has drained your energy.

The Search for the Perfect Chocolate Chip Cookie, by Gwen Steege (Storey). Take bad-day refuge in the kitchen! The ultimate bad-day good food.

Prayers & Graces from Dennis the Menace, by Hank Ketchum (Westminster/St. John). Dennis says, "And God, if you'll look at the instant replay, you'll see it wasn't my fault."

Bart Simpson's Guide to Life, by Bart Simpson and Matt Groening (HarperPerennial). Don't have a cow, man! Bart has advice for a bad day.

Alexander and the Terrible Horrible No Good Very Bad Day, by Judith Viorst (Atheneum). "He went to sleep with gum in his hair, and woke up with it in his mouth." And that was just the beginning.

Be a Clown, by Turk Pipkin (Workman). Complete with red rubber nose.

You Might Be a Redneck If..., by Jeff Foxworthy (Longstreet). A beer-belly laugh at the redneck in all of us.

Dancing Through Life with a Pair of Broken Heels, by Mickey and Cathy Guisewite (Bantam). Extremely short stories for the totally stressed. Cathy Guisewite is the creator of the comic-strip character "Cathy," the poster girl for bad days.

Ten Minutes to Relax (The Relaxation Group). Audiocassette with spoken instructions guiding you through relaxation techniques.

Who Needs God, by Rabbi Harold Kushner (Pocket Books). A gentle dose of faith (for any faith) on a bad day.

The Dance of Anger, by Dr. Harriet Goldhor Lerner (Harper). Turn bad-day anger into a constructive force for reshaping the day and your life.

You Can't Afford the Luxury of a Negative Thought, by John-Roger and Peter McWilliams (Prelude Press). Because you can't.

The Wholesale by Mail Catalogue (HarperCollins). When all else fails . . . shop. But this will help you avoid overspending, and avoid a bad-day mall experience.

The Phone Book. Pick it up and call a friend who listens. A bad day always gets better if you're not experiencing it alone.

Top Ten Foods to Eat on a Bad Day

1. Chocolate in any form
2. Chicken noodle soup
3. Macaroni and cheese
4. Mashed potatoes
5. French fries with ketchup
6. Popcorn
7. Banana splits
8. Peanut butter
9. Cinnamon toast
10. Chili

Movies to Rent on a Bad Day

All of Me

Annie Hall

The Big Chill

Blue Hawaii

Breakfast at Tiffany's

Easter Parade

E.T.

Fast Times at Ridgemont High

Funny Girl

The Good, the Bad, and the Ugly

It's a Wonderful Life

Just Between Friends

Manhattan

The Man with Two Brains

Meet Me in St. Louis

My Bodyguard

National Velvet

The Natural

9 to 5

Oh, God!

Oklahoma!

The Philadelphia Story

Pillow Talk

The Producers

Raising Arizona

Roxanne

Singin' in the Rain

Tootsie

Victor/Victoria

White Christmas

Who Framed Roger Rabbitt

Working Girl

Ten Ways to Turn Around a Bad Day

1. GET AHOLD OF YOURSELF — When you feel yourself spinning into that out of control bad-day cycle, stop and choose to halt the process. Get ahold of yourself! Choose not to let the cycle continue. You control your thoughts; they don't control you. You can stop this bad day from continuing.

2. PICTURE THE POSITIVE — Try a little "creative visualization." Sit down and picture how you would like this day to go. Be very specific with the scenarios you would like to see happen, rather than the way they seem to be headed. Some people say it helps to recall memories of a great day and the wonderful feelings of that day. If you can picture a positive situation, you can take yourself there.

3. CHOOSE A BAD-DAY FRIEND — A bad day seems much worse when you keep the thoughts, frustrations and disappointments to yourself. Pick a "bad-day friend" to call or go visit—preferably someone who isn't directly tied to the rotten events of the day. For example, if the bad day happened at work, you might want to pick a friend who doesn't know a soul at your office. Misery loves company, and a listening ear can be very comforting.

4. TRY THE SCARLETT O'HARA APPROACH — Think about it tomorrow! Sounds like an escapist plan? You bet. There are days when the best thing to do is take a bath, see a movie, eat a pan of brownies, re-roof the house . . . whatever it takes to forget the day's events. In many cases there is nothing you can do about the bad day anyway, so distract yourself and get past the past.

5. TAKE THE FOCUS OFF YOURSELF — Enough about you! Try doing something for someone else on your bad day. A favor or good deed for your spouse, your parents, your baby, your dog. You're guaranteed to feel better by making someone else's day instead of focusing on yours.

6. FAKE IT 'TIL YOU MAKE IT — Is it making you feel worse to announce to the world that you're having a bad day? Then knock it off. Fake it 'til you make it. Talk like life is great! Walk like you're on top of it all. The magic comes when you see how people respond. They will treat you like a winner, and you'll be contagious. One fashion tip for this one: Put on a bright-colored tie, sweater, whatever, to help give off a positive image of yourself even when you feel grey inside.

7. SEARCH FOR A REASON TO LAUGH — There has *got* to be something funny about this bad day! And laughter has an incredible effect on your body. It clears out your lungs, increases your heart-rate, and can help lower blood pressure. The best part is: Stress and laughter can't exist together in the human body. So if a good laugh comes, the stress has got to go. Laugh at the big blow-hard who made you so mad, laugh at yourself, laugh at how funny this bad day will seem in a month, or rent your favorite silly movie. Just laugh your way free of this bad day.

8. AVOID BAD-DAY JUNKIES — Do you know any of these people? They love to hear your bad-day news so they can point out to you just how truly horrible and miserable your life seems to be. Bad-day junkies will drain your energy rather than revitalize you. These are also people who love to repeat bad news, and they're usually not too discreet about how they tell your story or whom they tell. Even if you have a bad-day junkie in your family or close circle of friends, avoid this person for a day or two.

9. DO SOMETHING — Forget the chin-in-the-hand thinker pose. Get up and get moving. Just walking for twenty minutes will change your mood. So will taking action on something you've been procrastinating about. Clean out one drawer, fertilize your plants, put just a few pictures into that empty photo album. Being productive feels good.

10. WRITE YOURSELF A NOTE — Don't worry about grammar or spelling . . . but write a note to yourself about what happened today and what you can learn from it. You may have learned a tough lesson about yourself, or about a friend, or about

Life. Writing down your feelings will be a relief. It will help you sort out your confusing thoughts and free your mind to move on. Whether you keep the note in a diary or throw it out, this "love note" to yourself will help you write off a bad day.

About the Authors

Robyn Freedman Spizman outruns bad days by staying incredibly busy. She has written more than fifty-five parenting, educational and how-to books, including *The Thank-You Book* (Longstreet Press, 1994). A seasoned television personality, Robyn has appeared for the past ten years as "Super Mom" and a consumer reporter for WXIA-TV's "Noonday" in Atlanta. Robyn and her husband, Willy, have two children, Justin and Ali, and live in Atlanta, Georgia.

HAROLD ALAN PHOTOGRAPHY

Tracy Green learned to laugh in the face of bad days by spending a decade in the insanity of a TV newsroom. She is the executive producer of WXIA's "Noonday" talk show in Atlanta. She is the co-author of *52 Ways to Show Aging Parents You Care* (Thomas Nelson, 1992), a practical and inspirational guide to help families put love into action.